T0245016

# The
# Sisters

# The Sisters

## Jordan Windholz

**Black Ocean**
Boston · Chicago

Black Ocean
P.O. Box 52030
Boston, MA 02205
blackocean.org


Book Design by Janaka Stucky | janakastucky.com
Illustrations by Deanna Dorangrichia | dorangrichiaceramics.com


ISBN: 978-1-939568-92-2

Library of Congress Control Number: 2024934963


FIRST EDITION
Printed in Canada

See them. They are postures in lampblack, goldleaf, kermes, woad, but the intricate calligraphy of the illuminated manuscripts doesn't tell of how the sisters came to worship handfuls of loam, of how they praised the weightless world. It doesn't tell of what they desired and why they desired it. How the books have even forgotten they were sisters, and how the earth sought to fit its warmth to their bodies. How they were saints of their unbelief, their orisons nothing, nothing at all, and how they offered their unholy requests without compunction. Where might you find them, locate the secrets they held between their names and their naming? Where, having now only begun to look, will you turn, and to which sky will you lift your face, as if all its measured blue depended upon you turning toward its sun?

# Table of Contents

Notes & Acknowledgments

*for Hazel*

*and*

*for Bly,*

*sisters*

my sister calling
since the gold leaves have all
been lost, and you are at least
several and variegated

*Lisa Robertson*

# The Sisters in the Night

Together, but they didn't know how they arrived, in the center, or where they could imagine the center, of a dark forest, howls with teeth in them, a grey silence that ate their questions. They didn't even know if they were the villains, the wayward, the weird, the witches cursed to conjure sprites and devilish curs, if they were an ancient magic feeding saplings into a heretic bonfire, its pillar of wet, white smoke rising like a spell. The sky was black above them, stuck with stars that seemed the pinpricks of a bloodletting, their hot light hissing and steaming in the mists snaking through the woods. The moon was a sister of what they didn't know. They were not afraid. They had knives beneath their muslin, amethyst charms, a language that bent the world back to wishing. They imagined whatever was next was a perch with a nest of mottled eggs in its maw, a birthing of naked, flying forms or a tender meal for skulking cats.

# The Sisters in the Imagined Cities

In the atlases they were inking, cities took shape. A dot here.
A dot there. In each dot, lives of haphazard time. There were
cafés where they ate pastries that flaked then dissolved like
sugared snow on their tongues; cobblestone streets where
they listened to the clatter that they made climb the trellises
and harass the deep eaves of the avenues' rowhomes; sewers
that moaned with the city's lost children, and where, for an
hour or so, they joined that choir; plazas with their elaborate
clepsydras from which they stole a drink (and so also stole
two minutes and thirteen seconds); apothecaries where, in
shadows thick as the chuffing smoke of wildfires, they bartered
two porcelain keys for brown bottles of poisons and cloying
potions. In the cities they were drawing, there were empty
cathedrals whose limestone buttresses dissolved in the rain,
cities in which they lit beeswax votives and watched as the
priests of routine pinched each wick and inhaled each wisp.
There were lobbies of neon that hummed their vacancies
along desolate highways, newsstands whose tabloids yellowed
in a town bored of gossip. Ziggurats seemed to tug skies down
to the horizons. There were also arcades where machines
chewed up dimes, clanged and clamored and blared into the
thousand other small corners of bisecting alleys identical to
every other city. And then there was the final city that had
lost its charter, overgrown, a tangle of wye oaks and ivy, its

granite facades crumbling beneath a sun less ancient than permanent, its wash of light a tide of time scouring memories from monuments, each venerable figure a testimony of what is yet to be lost to its name.

# The Sisters in the Emperor's Gardens

Through the stone arch and down stone steps, they entered a menagerie of unmade beasts. The giraffe of privet goitered and bloated, the lion shaggy and spined, more porcupine than predator, and a massive twiggy skeleton twisted into some amphibious fauna, which they assumed was once a regal elephant. A giant sparrow netted by vines, chewed through by beetles, and skewered by grassy stalks was a nest for the wind. These gardens were once a place for the royal one to unfix himself from his regimented habit, to make his body a clock for thought when the court's magicians with their sinking bowls sought to plot too strictly his steps. Lost already to the overgrowth, the sisters didn't have much to think about, and so they circled through the spiraling paths, plinked stones in crumbling fountains now pocked with pools of rainwater, stood still and stared at the garden's pillars amid the parterre. They listened and thought how, without the small talk of songbirds or the crunch and shuffle of the royal one's walks, silence sounded like time trying to hear its heartbeat, which, of course, it did not have.

# The Sisters and their Automaton

When their first automaton lost its balance and fell down the stairs, they stood above its mass of angles and dents and saw visions of fire as its chittering and whirs slowed and then seized. Their second automaton was too much of a bore. It pressed its aluminum head against the bay window and sighed when it rained. The sisters got tired of rolling their eyes at its little performances of grief that it had learned from observing the mourners exiting and entering the funeral home across the street. When they buried it, it wouldn't stop eulogizing itself, and so the sisters felt compelled to rush their heaping of the final slaps of dirt until its sobs grew silent. The third automaton never became more than an idea, and so, it remained perfect in its hypothetical postures, its speculative comportment. The fourth automaton was their favorite, and its loss disturbed them greatly, so much so that the fifth automaton spent most of its time rousing the sisters from their depressive episodes, coaxing them from their beds and into their workshop, where they might once again proceed with the labor that was, and still is, ever before them.

# The Sisters Separated

Because they didn't know they were sisters, they passed each other on the streets as they went to work, then home, then back again. In their apartments, they, exhausted, would sink their separate heads into their separate pillows, but they would not, because they could not, sleep. They would stare at the edges of the bedroom's crenulated dark, trying to shake out of their minds the insistent buzz of the day's glass minutes. At times, they felt compelled to whisper pleas into the opportunity of the night. These were not prayers. Every so often, they would murmur the same words at the same time, or the rhythm of their breathing would synchronize for a cycle or two. Nothing manifested out of such serendipity. They would not even think to name what they felt as loneliness; feeling merely welled up in them until the brinks of their bodies became thin, almost translucent. In their most sleepless of nights, they would reach their hands out, as if into that need, as the absent air poured like moonlight right through them.

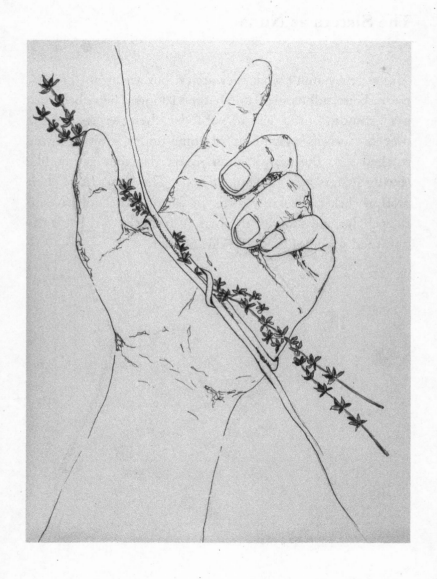

# The Sisters as Nuns

And so, they aren't what they aren't, but are errant prayers, error's heirs, tidbits and habits, clothed doors. Their obedience is a testimony of the right to exit today, their poverty a giving over as much as a giving up or going under, a bit of thyme stitched into the clove's hitch. Every day they gather like cloying oysters at a convenient hour. The lit wicks of their motives flicker like whispers in the ear of god. They have no rulers. They are superior mothers. What lives in them is the upturned sound of an upside-down letter.

# The Sisters Diving

They were ever-dazed in their diving bells, for you can only go so deep with your head inside a bubble of air, with your feet chained to an elemental weight tugging your buoyancy below what's below. They knew this, so when their air expired, and their lungs heaved like a field exhaling its color to tinder in August heat, and the water entered their mouths like a demon hot for its hell, the shock they felt was not at death's quick knock but at the surprise of, well, living without the burden of breathing. They walked across sands contoured by thermohaline currents, watched as mantas spun above like vultures in an alien sky, felt the chill of shadow as whales the shapes of clouds sucked in krill. At these depths, they did not envy the periodic surfacing of porpoises or of those fish that sought sun, found flight, speared light with their glittering skins. They only wanted descent, so they crawled over coral, cutting their knees, ignored the frenzy of sharks, the shifting eels, slid down continental shelves, and tiptoed to the edges of trenches, peered deep into the abyssal breach, into the dark-seeing eyes of sea goblins, watched as life streaked out in ribbons, in translucent pulsing spheres, canopies of stinging filaments, out of that absence, another, and out of another absence, more.

# The Sisters as Points of Infinite Regression

Imagine the painting is itself a kind of looking, turning its back on its gallery. Or imagine: a calamity of wind disperses, or no, it is a flock blowing weather toward you. A hand waves goodbye. It is a hand waving hello.

# The Sisters as Captains of Industry

They fed pig iron into forges, poured ore into molds, melted and minted their gold. They shrugged at the sweat of the beaters, dabbed their philtrums with silk, blinked and breathed as the chuffs of coal-black smoke seemed to give shape to their capital's invisible rise. They were surprised at how good it felt to be evil, to love the love of money. How benign they seemed because they smiled, had lovely families. In bespoke suits, they posed for portraits that would hang in the future halls of their philanthropy. At breakfast, on their verandas, luxuriating in the life of a dream that dreamed them, they thought how fantastic it was to have hoisted themselves up from nothing with nothing but the helping hand of wealth.

# The Sisters Hiding

If, at this particular moment, a traveler were wandering through here—there isn't—what would they see? Would they notice how the twilight settles like fine dust on this glen, that dale, this copse, and then another, how a river rushes through its hisses and gurgles into the silence distance makes of listening? Would they check their map to affirm how lost they were only to apprehend that the great cloud billowing inside them was a loneliness defying a name? And as they walk on, unsure if the branches snapping betrayed two bodies sneaking away from disclosure, if the wind's wooshing was instead—could it be?—the shushing of two sisters—no, impossible in this wilderness—would deer start and halt into their animal attention, grasses in their twitching snouts, dirt dropping from white tendrils and nubby roots? Would an owl hoot then, startling these inquiries into resolve? And what would they do when it stopped hooting and the evening was once again an ear that was less hearing than watching?

# The Sisters on the Moon

The earth was a pearl between the teeth of an immense, obsidian skull. Here, silence seemed a living thing that had a name for them. You wouldn't think you could breathe, they thought, for that is what they had been told. It was harder, to be sure, but after a few hours, their labored gasps became routine. As for the landscape, it wasn't much to look at or to even think about. Just grey and grey and grey and grey that eventually curved into the infinite black. All of their wonder, all of the songs and poems they had memorized, all of the fables and myths they had been told by parents, all of those nursery rhymes about this globe of cratered gleaming, seemed to float right out of their heads, inch by inch, each time they blinked. Spinning along in that lunar orbit, they needed new words to lend patina to pallor. This one thing could be said, however: it was a good place for hop-scotch, for its rocks, easily held, could be flung for some distance, and with minimal effort, they could skip further than they had ever dreamed possible on those summer days on earth, when long grasses bent in breezes, and the sunlight transformed everything but itself into a thing to see.

# The Sisters in a Forgotten Library

The sisters opened a book, surprised to see its words migrating as if the letters were iron filings and some invisible, hovering magnet moved laterally above them. They looked closer: mites, which, they soon discovered, had eaten the very ink off the pages. As they hibernated and huddled, the mites created a strange, new grammar, no more permanent than the atmospheres of their dream cycles. But then the sisters' awe at the voraciousness of this colony sank into the terror of a revelation. They turned to the book's last page. More mites scrambling, chomping. They saw the final gobble of the last word of what one could only imagine was some ancient moral, a final confession of an unholy saint, a record of a mighty queen's conquests, or an index to the diaries of Renaissance courtesans, now disappearing—*ist, st, t,* .

# The Sisters as Regicides

It didn't surprise them, exactly, how cleanly the blade slipped between the bones of his neck, how, with just the slightest heft of their bodies on the hilt, his screaming—like a child's, really—cratered into a singular whimper, then a wheeze. With his head off, the King—but was it right to call him that now?— was nothing more than what all corpses are: a heap of flesh, a sinewy mess, time's ragged lace. It was a mistake, they had come to realize, to allow him the Tyrian purple stole of his coronation. They had been sentimental, had pitied the old man. Splayed across the platform, it sopped up the blood like a leech. It was ruined. Upon the scaffold, they understood why it is one wears a crown. They dipped their hands in the crimson coagulating around their feet and placed their sticky palms over their hearts. When they held up his head, the crowd cheered. Their fingers clutching its wispy hair, it was heavy, but not too heavy, not too heavy.

# The Sisters as Fragments

How is it they? An up. The writing of. Suffering infinite.
Golden infant. But not an. Was a boy. A fuscia in their
meaning. An accident. An arrival. What another called an
edge. An etching. Not them. A turning toward. Said to. Oh,
if only. A brick. Them. As the weight of. A tree in the brain.
A heaving through. Yes, love, this is what. A further. To know
or not, but to. A feeling out. Into, but not never. Is one way.
Not ever. Not gone.

# The Sisters in a Hockney Painting

They are the pink arms of summer. They are the diving board hot for the splash. They are the absent yellows. Look at me, David, they are saying. Let me be your David. Let me be your patio. They are Joe by the Green Window. They are the pleasant, eclectic décor. They are Johnny and Lindsay. They are the palms and shrubs all too green. They are so many ways of looking all at once. They almost see the sun in them. Everywhere the water, and a body sliding through, sliding through a body like it's the coolness of a pool.

# The Sisters as Vampires

You invite them in. You aren't supposed to, you know this, and you tell yourself you're not supposed to even as the thoughts of *come in come in come in* rumble in your gut, and you do, you do, you invite them in. But not much happens after that. The *what if* pumping of your adrenaline falls back to the *this this this* of your heartbeat, and what was opening in you still opens, but like a flower wilting into its bloom. It isn't like they don't do vampire things. They watch you sleep. They breathe on your neck as they run their noses across its nape. They levitate. They refuse to open the curtains, keep them pinched with clothespins. And they do not leave. Every night, they drink and they drink and they drink. First, it's wine. Then gin. Then whiskey. Then it's wine again. As soon as their tongues start slipping on their sentences, they tell you a story. It's always the same story. It's about a peasant boy, about how, one day, he wandered into the forest in pursuit of a chicken that escaped from its yard, or no, no, they say, it was a goat bleating into the dusk, or no, the other corrects her sister, it was a girl from the village, and he didn't wander. They never slur their words at this next part. They run their long nails against the lips of their glasses as they tell of how the whole village searched for him all day and all night, all day and all night, for a week and another, how they lit fires that inevitably dwindled to ash heaps, murmured prayers into their hands, how they filled the air with their wailing because they believed the sky held a god whose tongue wasn't clipped, one whose ears were not sewn shut. They tell of how they did not find a bit of him, not one of his shoes, not a thumb, not a strand of hair, not even a tooth.

# The Sisters as Horses

Think: when are they not galloping through the myth America has made of them? Where have you seen them before you have seen them? What accidents of nature, of fortune, of fickle cells fitting themselves to hoof and fetlock, coronet and cannon, pastern and poll, withers, crest, croup, muzzle, and tail—what luck tricks itself into such muscled velvet? The sisters, of course, being horses, did not contemplate such questions. They ate grasses, fixed their wet eyes west as the sun set. They did not feel human nonsense. They did not imagine that a horizon hid their true home. No. They simply bedded down in the fields, which were no more or less theirs, the stars in their heads merely their stars.

# The Sisters as Two Among the Many

People are waking up to being people again, and the sisters, too, are pouring their coffee and eating their eggs. There is a feeling that rises in them that makes them want to say what the light is, but it is just the light. The air warps into the chemistry of breathing, and they are, for now, breathing the warped air. When they think back on this day, it will be a kind of accident. They will have wanted to remember a day this meaningless, a day that they lived in without it having to have been a day like any other, without it having to be a day unlike every other, the light just so on the sills, the wind making a door of itself through the streets.

# The Sisters on a Sudden Hill

Green, they say, their hill is green, and blue, they see the sky is blue. The clouds, they know, are shapes geometry does not conceive. Deep below their feet, the earth aggregates its extinctions into the lush hum of its millennia, and the sunlight warms them on their sudden hill. The sunlight is a local tuning. The sunlight is hot. They sit beneath their orange tree and nap amid the sound of the plump fruit dropping and rolling on its way.

# The Sisters as Their Disappearance

They had fled, and their vanishing was a gravity that bent their parents' routines into orbits of sorrow. But they left a note. It read,

> Because we can never be anything but your children, we have always been a disappearance, a memory surfacing. We have always been going, would always be gone. If it helps, enter each night with your head open. Try to swallow what will never be there so that you might know what it is to make a ritual of hunger. Lie in your bed and think of the stars, how what is already lost to time comes to plot the sailor's wandering homeward, how the sailor wanders, how the sea heaves, how the horizon is always a continent receding. Then, as you drift into sleep, pretend your heart is a beast you are starving into its instinct. When you can feel its ribs through its slick coat, let it eat freely. Let it eat. Let it eat.

Their parents pinned the note to the fridge. What else was there to do with such a thing? At first, they read it every day for weeks, but then they became numb to its dicta, came to stare at its scrawl as if it were a photograph fading into the moment it was meant to recall. It always remained unbearable for them, how even when they held each other in their bed they knew they were holding a comfort that was pregnant with the horror of their loss. How they cried every day. They cried, and they could not stop, for they had no daughters to protect from the humiliation of their grief.

# The Sisters in an Immense Expanse

It was hard to notice them, but they were there among the windswept hills of glacial silt that vein these plains and that cascade into horizons that make your scrutiny an attention without end.

# The Sisters After the Day They Die

Because of an editing error, after they die, the sisters incorrectly incorporate a season into every *however*, every *further*, every *giving over*. You look to September, and there, a little bit of a coffin. You look at Friday, and the passenger of disappointment creates a daily protest. The family car slides into a movie about a specific hurt. The sisters think about it quite often as they knit pictures of themselves into television shows. Because their disappointment appears like diesel inside a museum, their faces incompletely change, disclosing misidentified artists, columns of rendered emissions, points in felt time. Last year's gorge is a bridge, and they, the sisters, are a February in suspension. It is not the case that we all turn to years. The sisters disclose more about the publicly listed, privately owned, naked officials traded in exhibitions for tourists, how it was June when the low power opposed America's focused reducing of community. It is often a managed losing into which you, too, will be included. That's kind of something.

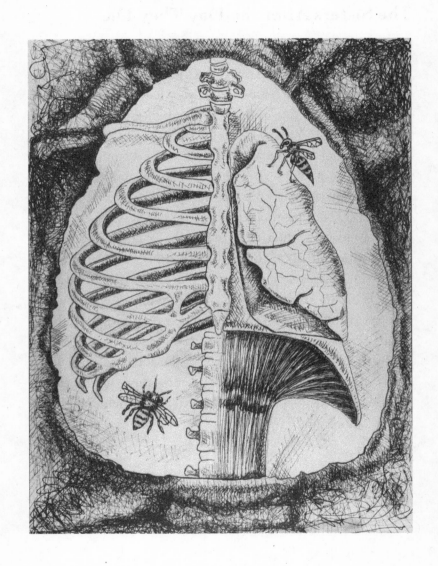

# The Sisters as Ghosts

Haunting was such boring work, and it didn't take long before they questioned why it was they were living the stories that the sobbing and fearful wrote to make sense of the grave. How presumptuous to assume ghosts had nothing better to do than fling a few books across a room, bang doors, breathe on the smalls of backs. They did all these things at first, of course. But the world was too full of new experiences, which were just old ones that had shed their familiarity. Remembering a spring day when some bees welted their bodies and ballooned their eyes shut, they floated outside, harassed a hive in the yard, and marveled at how the swarm spun in their chests in a honey-drunk rage, and then, as if slipping into the amnesia of a suddenly recollected routine, the bees dispersed out their eyes, their noses, their mouths, their elbows, their bellies, and once again groomed themselves in pollen and gorged themselves with nectar. Instead of climbing trees, the sisters sat inside an oak, felt the pull and push of the pith through their vaporous spines. They felt the heartwood tighten. They suspended and stretched themselves thin through rock strata, their heads deep in the Cambrian, their toes lengthening out across the Permian and pushing up into soil like tulip bulbs rolling into bloom. Their days went on like this until what remained was the enduring question of what they were. They probed their substanceless forms with substanceless fingers, contemplated the unlogic of spectral physics. Day turned into day and into day, and their questions of unbeing became a flood that floated their every thought until they were perpetually living in that moment of searching for the right word, of standing forever on that edge of hoping that what they were feeling would exorcise their language of its alphabet, that whatever was left of them would séance what they were out of what they were.

# The Sisters as the History of Blue

Like a dragonfly dipping the tip of its tail on the hood of a hot car, you have to be a lover of likenesses to see them. The sky is like the sea, a glass's looking. The sister like a sister. Say you place blue between them. What are they now? A tilting, perhaps. A petal in shade. A coast flowering in ice. You might say there is a wind in the glacier, a light in the wind. The iceberg in the sea, the sky in the light. You might say. What would you? They are so green with likeness, you have to look at them to see it. The dragonfly still on a green stalk flickers into the speed of a color. The sky calving into the sea, the sea so much vapor cooling into clouds. They are so blue with difference, you have to look at them to forget. What you cannot see is blue, like forgetting. Or the dragonflies unzipping the air. You have to look to see. Do you? Do you look?

# The Sisters in the Dream of a Giant

With their nervous and digestive systems a fibrous tangle, a giant's dreams are kaleidoscopic conjurations; the slightest alimentary roiling cascades into anamorphic displays. So they never knew at any given moment what shape they might take. Once, they manifested as chimeras, their wings taut and fleshy, their talons gore-stained, their eyes unspeaking. Another time, they seemed to be some kind of sponge, gorging and disgorging on the seafloor. And even when they malformed into something closer to human, they never knew what mutations might occur. Their eyes might retreat into their faces like hermit crabs clinking into their shells, their mouths migrate to their bellies and speak in an elaborate rhythm of belches and hiccups. But now, and quite suddenly, they had precipitated out of their shapes as a lurching, tentacled slime and into sisters again, and so they took each other's hands, stepped into a meadow just now unfolding before them in greening grasses and the sun-jealous neon of blossoms. Even as they frolicked, they knew they were merely the perturbations of a brain fumigated by the vapors of bowels, the huffing smoke of the crunched bones and simmering blood of gnashed peasants boiling in a gut. And still, they frolicked, frolicked and sang. They picked a flower, and then they picked another.

# The Sisters as the Last Page of a Book

What is it to be forever the end? What is it to live a life antic-
ipating a turning? Any moment now, you think, until, at last,
that moment does not come. Like sheaves of wheat tossed on
wagons, they were always between a harvest and a threshing.
Like all final things, they made a story of their origin. There
was a god who fixed them into a form and another who would
breathe them into life. How much of them was remembering
what came before, how much forgetting? You want to make
sense of this world, they thought, and so you look for a
place to begin. You want to make sense of it. Pressed and
fixed firmly into the day of the page, they kept thinking, what
would become a becoming, make what's last everlasting, a last
and longing never, an only ever, ever always if?

# The Sisters as Hunters

They knew the trick. They had to be quiet. Flat on their bellies, skin pressed to the saccharine of desiccated leaves, they were the mist rising from the forest floor and creeping into dawn's shadow-thick light. Their brain knocked hard in their heads. They had to make death a secret the arrow whispers to the deer. They had to make death, shoulder their spears between the boar's ribs and let the wound gurgle and sputter. They had to soak their hands in the gore as they flayed the beast and dressed the meat. They had to eat, and so they hunted. They had to hunt, and so they ate. At night, the dark would swell with screeching, and they would wrap themselves in that noise as if it were a fur blanket. They would fall asleep as the fire sizzled and snapped at the animal grease still dripping from the spit, slip into sleep with their bellies fat, their dreaming dizzy with the fury of wasps crushed into wine.

# The Sisters in the Desert West

Coyotes yip, and the night opens into a bright coolness. They fall asleep under the stars, which are meaningless, if beautiful. There are so many.

# The Sisters as the Sky

To be the vault of dread, a river of stars, the blue imperium that waking wakes to, the night that would forget you, the threshold where air diffuses into atmosphere, the blinded eye of fate's seer, Shakespeare's welkin, the ruin of the ramshackle, tumbledown dusk, the furnace of dawn—they simply had to be. On Tuesday, they picked a plain, thundered, became a little rain seceding from its storm. On Wednesday, they bled themselves of color, became an emptiness, a glimmering region, some wasted acres. All of their life was a kind of focusing, a choosing of accidents, a whether or not.

# The Sisters as Sisters

Their hearts of glass were filled with sand, their dunes sculpted by the blood's shifting winds. Their hearts of blood were brined in salt, their tides the swells of tearless mothers who would not turn from catastrophe. Each had a story they would tell of each other. Each had a story they would tell of themselves. Each had a story they would not tell, a kind of melody played on the brain's clavier. They knew each other as strangers know the city they share, how one morning a season shifts, a street cools beneath an autumn evening's fog. How after it rains, you open a window. They knew each other like neighbors listening to each other through the wall, their ears like lips about to kiss. They knew each other like playing children understand each other as familiars, how, as in the middle of playing pretend, they become a house they can properly haunt, how, in that moment, a movement they might be and might become.

# The Sister as Co-conspirators

The night drops into a pen. How is that love? It is not windy at all, though some flags are up. Some look like vines, some look like ivy, some look like grass. There are trees. The sisters are somewhere, some anywhere, some elsewhere where they are girls, girls playing a song and singing to their dogs. The earth is quiet and very lonely.

# The Sisters and the Sea

The waves dug their teeth into the bow of their little boat, the salt gnawing on the oarlocks. It had been a week. Last night they welcomed the storm for its rain that they might drink, and yes, they welcomed it too that they might raise their fists to the thunder, that voice without a mouth. Even as they hooted and roared, they knew the boat would sink. In the calm of the morning, delirious with their lack of sleep, they thought that if their circumstance had not been a heavy fact, they might hold it in their mind as a motto, an image that might, like an anchor, set a limit to, in another life, their drifting in and out of rooms, where, lit by their smoldering boredom, they would dawdle below the stifled smiles of adults that were less impressed with what they were becoming than marveling at how quickly they could transform into mannequins of accomplishment. The water slapped the starboard, sending a fine spray into their faces. Now resigned to the fate of the sea-soaked and shipwrecked, the dreams of the drowned, they peered over the side, glimpsed silver darts shimmering, imagined what it is to fall into depths of blue, to disappear only then to rise as a trick of light.

# The Sisters in the Attic

They were not yet crusted in dust, and so they imagined them-
selves as memories or dreams, as the ravenous thoughts of
the house, rising and circling like vultures. They would stomp
and growl, jump and pound on the floor. They heard the lilt
of human questions from below, their parents querying after
them. They didn't have long before they were discovered,
before they must be girls again. One put on a wig that she
might practice tearing out her hair, the other a wedding gown
that she might rehearse its tattering, make of it a lantern for
the flame her body would be. They placed glass bowls to their
ears, whispered into them. When they heard the creak of the
attic door opening, they dropped them to the floor, the globes
shattering, their secrets scattering, and so, safe.

# The Sisters as Insects

They could disappear with the faintest breeze, just open their wings, just tilt into air. They could munch a leaf. It was lovely to be anonymous, another buzz, a scratching click in a world of so much noise.

# The Sisters as Cardinals

Not as flames alight in pines, not as the wind cut open by the wing's red blade, and not as the blood-stained cathedral built around the holy air of an absent idol. No. They were red as true north. They were the color of the lost ones finding their way, the color of the wolf's howling hunger, of the ear of the rabbit's fear. They perched where they would. They threaded their bodies through the seeing of children, stitched awe into their vanishing. What is wind but a nerve, their bodies bright ideas the sky thinks and forgets? They were marvelous, truly. Hopping from stone to ground, from branch to branch, they wondered at running, puzzled over the leg's thudding rescue of the human's falling form again and again, again and again. They marveled, but not too long, their black eyes a shining knowing. This is what it is to be, to see in splendor a mirrored splendor. They knew what it was to wear the heat of the heartbeat on their beating wings. See how they spread them. See what it is to be the high priests of a religion where the gods themselves flagellate, catechize, repent before these, their altars of red.

# The Sisters at the Great River

It is not thinking of them as it sidles past the golden-tasseled, earth-shocked rows of corn. The sun is not an echo of light in the ear of it. It is not listening to them, how small they are, how so very small. The river is not exiting weather, not a which way, not a glitch of water, not either or after, not a tear or a tearing, a wet fear, a rushing growing. The sisters stand on its muddy bank. They sit and dip their toes in. The river says the water, the water says the river is. The sisters wade into it, the cool of it coiling around their thighs. They step deeper. Debris drifts downriver, and they step deeper still, and deeper still, until the current takes them. Then the dusk. Then the river being.

# The Sisters on a Country Road

Where comes that violence born of boredom, the man or boy who swerves his truck out of its lane in the night to strike the fox now stunned in the sudden, roaring brightness? Is it, like a cloud, a condensing, or like a wind, a pressure shifting? Is it whim or whimsy or whimper? The sisters stood on the side of the road staring at the rusty pelt, its organs inky in the unspeakable heat. A breeze stirred its fur. It was not hard to imagine it in its den, asleep in its animal sleep, oblivious to that instant terror, to the veering machine on a road beckoning someone home.

# The Sisters in a Dream

You cannot wish yourself out of a dream. The snow falls. The air buckles, descends, shifts the landscape the falling flakes make. The snow falls, and it falls, sponges the heat straight from your blood until you slip into the dream the living dream of the dead. How blue they must be, how true to the decay that unfolds its petals in each cell. You cannot wish yourself out of a dream, they tell each other, noses to the window, as they watch the snow, how it falls, how this white world is all the whiter because of the dead, dead, dead it buries.

# The Sisters as Lies

Half of all squids speak French, the sisters read, and a third of all facts are acts of faith the reasoning few imbue with their esoteric rituals of data. A quarter of all owls are pleas fetal mice make to forestall their births, and a third of all words are derived from the happenstance glyphs of murmurating warblers. There is no truth a lie can't shape. It's all in their books, which they gather now, and dump into a mound. It's all in their books, onto which they drop a furious match. It sparks the pile of pages into a velvet heat. The fire roars like a heresy set down by a gaggle of Puritans. It seethes like the very sin the sermons say are pressed beneath their frocks. How many men have told them what it is to know, have told them that their bodies were a story they had to inherit? Their faces flicker into a smile as the blaze blazes like Archimedes' burning glass. How reckless, they will be told, how evil. But they know now. Nature has her witnesses. The fire is only the air alive with what it knows.

# The Sisters as Red Riding Hood

The red comes after. Their cowls are first blue, or they are green, or they are a remarkable yellow shining through its dye. Every day, the hard work. For hours, they lop open wolves, searching their bellies for the mothers of their mothers. Every day, they whet the axe blade. Within some grove, the muted echoes, the thwack, drag, and thwack. For hours, they burn entrails, seek a premonition in the smoke. They pack cups full of ash, pick out pieces of bone. They line their huts with hundreds of these cups. They wash their hands in the creek, break their bread. They eat. The woodsmen the next town over tell stories about them, how they are always on a journey, heading for a home. The children fashion little dolls of flax and wool, dip them in the broth of madder root. Those rustics believe that sharing little myths about those girls will insulate them in the safety of story. But we—we know to lock our doors. The things we tell you before you fall asleep, dear ones, are not meant to usher you into the dark halls of slumber. We do not tell you them so that you would learn the proper place to harbor your fear. The silks you feel brushing your face are not the gauzy curtains of dream. Do not close your eyes too tightly in the starlight.

# The Sisters and Their Story

They imagine their life as a story but it is not, it is not, it is knotted, sentences twisting into, twisting out, turning toward, until, until—

# The Sisters as Taxidermists

Is your grief a dove? Is it a crocheted pheasant? Is it a furred muscle? Is it a fig with a stinging thing nested in its nectar? Is your joy marsupial? Is each object a radiant posture? Is your hunger feathered with gills? No? Is it the ocelot? Is your worry a hedgehog? What is the Arctic fox of it? Is your desire a lamprey? Is it a shelled vessel, a tincture of flesh on a seabed? What is this, your breathing, your beating heart? Is it the shadow gliding on the night through the pines? Is it the pines?

# The Sisters as Poets

Their language makes a nest of its blah blah blah. Like cuckoos, they colonize someone else's sentiment, peck its shells clean. Blah blah blah: their soul is singing. In the mornings, they look for beauty, but there is only the sun again insinuating itself into something like the long shadows of hope. Despite their feathers, despite the mites that cling to their dirty wings, they are not birds anymore. Their talons lengthen. The head, finally on its pedestal and crowned with bays, has stopped crooning its sad little songs. When they close their eyes, an egg like a moon surfaces out of the sea.

# The Sisters as a Set of Arbitrary Instructions

You are told to pick up a piece of paper. You are told to stare at the paper as if it were a mirror. You are told to stare for five minutes. You are told to collect pencil shavings into a little mound next to the paper. You are told to smudge your finger in the graphite of the pile. You are told to look again at the paper, to trace the reflection you do not see there. You are told to now take the cup of water that has been on the table for three days. You are told to slowly drip the water onto the paper until it is a perfectly bluish pulp. You are told to open the windows, to invite the season's swelter into this room. You are told to watch the paper dry, to place your face over it, and to huff the dehydrating air above its slowly constituting surface. You are told that the paper before you is now ready for whatever will be. You are told that you do not believe this. You do not believe this.

# The Sisters in the Present

So much of what *is* lost is, simply. They can't even remember their great-grandmothers' middle names. Only the living might call this a tragedy. Still, there is a bee in their sorrow, a wasp inside their joy. There is another insect they cannot name, but it is not inside anything. Its shadow rests on their hand that rests on the table in the cool of the day. They had placed the vase of alstroemeria there, and it persists. It is a life that does not require their witness. The afternoon cascades through it, an hour, and another. They can barely recall what yesterday was like, what epiphanies displaced their doings between lunch and dinner. Just outside the window, house sparrows and cardinals peck at the feeder.

# The Sisters as Pagans

They built themselves gods out of sticks, of drought-brittle grasses, of scraps of dried leaves. They built themselves little pyres, lit fires, imagined their martyrdoms as immolations into an immortal ash. There was nothing above they needed to pray to. But for their usefulness in mapping their stacking of stones, the stars were worthless to them. Lightning flashed, thunder crashed—they knew it was merely air being sucked through a hole made by the light, or maybe it was some new god clanging his gongs. Why worship such weightless things, they wondered, hands full of dirt. The earth would roll them into its urgency, their souls, in time, wedded to roots reaching down as far as the tree unfurling up. And so what? So what?

# The Sisters on the Day They Were Born

On the day they were born, the sisters became obsessed with anonymity. They became a blanched dilemma, a centerpiece vowing absence. It was not difficult to look back at their stories from the remains of their private influences. The world changed around them, and the years attended their joyous sense of untrammeled honesty. But they were dwindling. They were a disenchanted sorrow. The parables and allegories gilding their talismanic books broke into discourses that could not cleanse America's polluted skies and waters, and so they bent their mourning into a generosity, committed their lives to cosmic slop. They emerged failures and constructed their citizenship as an instrument of fraud, the dark buckling around them. Both acclaimed the minutes as the brutal wife of violent light. And they lingered. They made their bodies reinterpretations of the traditional material. They became creatures adapted to the bottom of a well. Where long histories were paths opening, they were contraband or dazzling strangers. They completely reinvented Pittsburgh. Everyone said they would always be remembered, but the future, which emerged as a complex of condolences, embedded its lasting hunger in the all-encompassing, all-embracing, and life-affirming stereotype of a version of 1985's chemical magic. So sentenced, the two made a swan of how they had survived, and they reinforced the counterfeit of all that appeared in print.

# The Sisters as the Space Behind Forgetting

As if susurrated from the silence from which a sound shaped into a word's sense first shudders, they lived beyond quietly. Their house: something like a polished fog. It was the bliss of obliviousness, the comfort of not knowing what you needed to remember and never would. There were acres, ever-rolling hills, ever-extending frontiers vanishing into their pioneer longing. Oh, do you see it, they would say, each and every morning, squinting into the dawn but never knowing what it was that they had longed to see. But oh those reds, oh those blues, oh those hues diffusing like so much expectation, oh so shapeless and wild without what was it, what was it, what was it?

# The Sisters in a New Myth

Dandelions shake their manes in the sun until the wind bleaches their locks and blows their crowns bald. The sisters stand in the center of a field and wonder. They test the breeze, fly a kite. They take a paper boat and set it in the creek, watch it bump and eddy in the fleeting rush and have no inkling to anchor their hearts to its odyssey. They plunk stones in gopher holes, snatch snakes by the tail. They sit naked in the sun and do not think to name a goddamn thing. Imagine everything's the same, except these sisters are lords to boys and bodies, to hunger and happiness. They trespass onto some old man's orchard. They pick dewy fruit from the trees and eat. Instead of a curse, praise.

# The Sisters During the War

How the human grease of each minute slipped through the
iron grates. There are lives that are lost, and there are lives
that are stolen. They don't know which they are living. How
they walked to school down wide streets among the women
in their blouses, faces wide as sunflowers, among men in
their oxford shirts contemplating the angles lurking in their
lawns. All their lives their nation was conducting a war it kept
forgetting it was conducting. Each day something like a thick
wafting rose out of their mouths, a symptomless symphony.
They wanted to tell themselves there was something they might
do, some weapon they might chain themselves to, anything to
believe that they were not also a glint in the war's animal eye.

# The Sisters as Grownups

Like so many chariots crashing into the sea, the gold bangles around their wrists flashed in the summer twilight. Their dresses, slick as snakeskin, clung to their hips, their backs, and their bellies, the sweat on their arms cooling and shining. This was dancing, they thought, drunk, finally, on so much wine. The fireflies pulsed and snuffed themselves out. They felt like children again, or what they, now grown, imagined children felt like, having let the future they had become fix itself into something firm, something like the ground below their feet upon which they twirled, eyes to the heavens, eyes to a night evacuating its light for whoever cared to look.

# The Sisters in the Catacombs

In the subterranean cities of the dead, everyone smoked. There were a few with marble pipes, cured cigars, opera lengths. But mostly, pedestrians took long drags on cigarettes. The smoke filled their heads, rose, dissipated out of their translucent skulls. Joints between their lips, the sisters waved their hands above their own heads, unsure of what floated out of them. They watched each other intently. Neither saw wisps spindling away into the humid shade. There only gathered haloes of light, quivering, flickering—but when they looked directly at them, or began to speak of their presence, they would disappear. So their conversation turned to a chorus of half sentences, exclamations, hoots, and other sounds hollowed out by a quick puff. Each had their own private certainty of this miracle as they walked together among the reanimated corpses, phantoms, the laughing ghouls, but they dared not speak of the shimmering just above them surely coronating their descent.

# The Sisters as Collaborators

The whales were diving. Their memory was an egg bereft of its wren. The sun was shining so brightly on the water. The salt was all the wind was thinking. The sisters were old houses creaking on the coast, lighthouses for shipwrecks. Do you hear them, the dolphins like mice, the dolphins like happy leopards? What is an ocean for? Swimming. Fishing. The blue dog running on the hot sand. The sisters read their book in the permanent noon. It is funny.

# The Sisters in an Unbidden Time

They had wanted to place their hands on each small thing.
The tree branches spasmed. It was a way of listening to the
weather, air shaken into petals. Their windows were other
mouths. They had built their life inside their bodies, neither
a wise nor unwise choice. On their balconies, or on their
stoops, they scrutinized the concrete and debris, anxious for a
new augury, one that might predict a true past. Fate is nothing
but what comes next, a horror's scope, they used to think. A
newspaper caught in the gate, what was it? They scuffed their
shoes against the inches of pavement. They thought of the
day as a kind of selection. The rain falling again, as if trying to
create an answer of itself, and the rain falling after.

# Notes & Acknowledgements

I'd like to thank the editors of the following publications where these poems first appeared, sometimes in alternate versions:

*Gold Wake Live*: "The Sisters on the Moon," "The Sisters in a Forgotten Library," "The Sisters Hiding," "The Sisters in the Desert West," and "The Sisters as Ghosts"

*Diagram*: "The Sisters as Captains of Industry" and "The Sisters in the Dream of a Giant"

*Tupelo Quarterly*: "The Sisters as Lies" and "The Sisters as Sisters"

*the tiny journal*: "The Sisters in the Night," "The Sisters as Vampires," and "The Sisters as Red Riding Hood"

*Seneca Review*: "The Sisters as the History of Blue"

The epigraph of the book comes from Lisa Robertson's "How to Judge," from *Debbie: An Epic*, New Star Books, 1997.

Thank you Janaka and Carrie for your care and attention to these poems, and for giving them a home.

Thank you Deanna Dorangrichia for your wondrous illustrations. I couldn't have imagined them, but I am so grateful you could.

Written first as bedtime stories for my daughters, these poems were largely private affairs until they weren't. I owe almost everything to Erin Ryan for her attentive reading and care, and for her urging me to put them out in the world. She is my first and last.

Michael Flatt provided invaluable insights and suggestions as this manuscript developed. I learn so much from him and from his poetry.

Thank you Lucas and Rivers for your abiding friendships, and for always asking to read my poems.

I'd like to thank my departmental colleagues at Shippensburg University, especially Nicole Santalucia, who has always championed my work. I love her poetry so, so much. You should read it.

The bulk of this manuscript came into being through the Carlisle Writers Group. It would not exist without the care, attention, enthusiasm, and critique of all who participated in it. Jon Dubow and Freya Gibbon began and sustained this writing community. They opened their home and brought us all together. "The Sisters as Two Among the Many" is for Jon, who tempered many of these poems' excesses and saw the truer poem in each one. "The Sisters as Nuns" is for Freya, who was always attuned to where the poems worked and how to strengthen them; she especially strengthened this one. Thank you Rob Lesman, Tara Stillions Whitehead, Ana María Moraña, Zack Grabosky, and Jaime Juarez for sharing your writing and for reading mine. I owe you all a great debt.

My family has and continues to sustain me in all the ways that make poems possible. Mom, Dad, Jan, Don, Jo, Colby, Alyssa, Rachel, Tim, Kyle, and Nikki: how could I ask for more? You are blessings upon blessings.

Beyond being the immediate audience for these poems, my daughters collaborated with me on two of them. Bly co-authored "The Sisters as Co-conspirators," and Hazel co-authored "The Sisters as Collaborators." Both "The Sisters after the Day They Die" and "The Sisters on the Day They Were Born" were composed of found language. Except for the titular phrase, the words of each are drawn and recomposed from corrections and retractions (for the former) and obituaries (for the latter) published in *The New York Times* on the respective dates of my daughters' births.

Hazel and Bly, the possibilities that you are, and that you continue to be, made these poems possible. I hope you like some of them. I love each of you very much, and I will never stop. Always remember you are sisters.